RELIGIOUS CONVICTION AND THE 'NEW MAGNA CARTA'

Pervaiz Ahmad Buttar
and
Lynette Joy Mattingley

CENTRE FOR SOUTHEAST ASIAN STUDIES

OCCASIONAL PAPER
No. 24

General Editor: Bob Hering

ISSN 0159-4915

National Library of Australia Cataloguing in Publication Data

Buttar, Pervaiz Ahmad.
Religious conviction and the New Magna Carta.

ISBN 0 86443 221 6.

1. Religious liberty — Australia. 2. Civil rights — Australia. 3. Australia — Constitutional Law. 4. Religious liberty — Asia, Southeastern. I. Mattingley, Lynette Joy. II. James Cook University of North Queensland. Centre for Southeast Asian Studies. III. Title. (Series: Occasional paper (James Cook University of North Queensland. Centre for Southeast Asian Studies); no. 24).

342.94'0852

Wholly set up and printed within the University

James Cook University
Townsville Qld 4811
Australia

RELIGIOUS CONVICTION AND THE 'NEW MAGNA CARTA'

RELIGIOUS CONVICTION AND THE 'NEW MAGNA CARTA'

Mr PERVAIZ AHMAD BUTTAR, LL.M.(London)[1]

Mrs LYNETTE JOY MATTINGLEY, LL.B.(Hons)(Q.I.T.)[2]

> "**116.** The Commonwealth shall not make any law for establishing any religion, or for imposing any religious observance, or for prohibiting the free exercise of any religion, and no religious test shall be required as a qualification for any office or public trust under the Commonwealth."
>
> The Australian Federal Constitution

With these words the Australian Constitution enshrines the "freedom of religion". Apart from Section 116 it also refers to "Almighty God" in the preamble to the Constitution. It is suggested that these two references to "religion" may be paradoxical but were intended to satisfy the secularists, the non-conformists as well as the mainstream religious groups.[3] Although modelled upon the First Amendment of the U.S.

---

1. Barrister of the Supreme Court of NSW, Advocate Supreme Court of Pakistan, Lecturer in Commercial Law, James Cook University.

2. Solicitor of the Supreme Court of QLD, Tutor in Commercial Law, James Cook University.

3. Discrimination & Religious Conviction, NSW Anti-discrimination Board 1984.

Constitution the freedom in Section 116 stands alone. Since the section appears in a chapter entitled "The States", it is suggested that Section 116 was intended to keep the Commonwealth out of the religious field and only the States had the power to legislate regarding religion.[4] Further proposals to amend Section 116 to extend its coverage to the States failed in a referendum in 1944.

The fact remains that the only State that provides a constitutional religious guarantee is Tasmania. Section 46 of the Tasmanian Constitution Act 1934 provides a positive guarantee of practice of religion. This is however subject to public order and morality and can be overridden by any other Act of the Tasmanian Parliament.

A. Free Exercise of Religion

What do the words "free exercise of religion" in Section 116, confer upon a citizen? During the second world war, this freedom was interpreted not to include being a Jehovah's Witness. The High Court also held that Section 116 did not prevent the enactment of laws prohibiting the advocacy of pacifism even though it was based upon a religious conviction. This issue arose when the Commonwealth dissolved the Witnesses and seized their property after declaring them to be subversive bodies prejudicial to the defence of the Commonwealth. Nevertheless the High Court held the

---

4. R. Ely, Unto God and Caesar: Religious Issues in the Emerging Commonwealth 1891-1906, Melbourne University, Melbourne 1976. It has been recently noted in the Grace Bible Church Inc. v. Reedman (1984) 54 ALR 571 that nothing prevents a State Parliament from legislating to interfere with the religious freedom.

regulations under which they had been banned, as invalid.[5] In an earlier case in 1912 the High Court took a narrow view of the word "exercise" equating it with the word "practice" and it was interpreted to mean freedom to attend "the church of your choice."[6] The High Court in this case held that a Commonwealth law "conscripting" male persons for military service was not in breach of Section 116 despite its application to persons whose religious belief's forbade the bearing of arms. The section will not, however, prevent the exercise of a Court's jurisdiction under matrimonial causes legislation if for example it is in the interest of the welfare of a minor.[7]

It must be stressed that Section 116 makes indefensible and discriminatory, any Federal legislation that singles out one religious group, while allowing another any comparable religious practices.[8] At present informal non-preferential or non-sectarian establishment of religion is not

---

5. Adelaide Company of Jehovah's Witnesses v. The Commonwealth (1943) 67 CLR 116. Though in 1951 the High Court held that the Communist Party Dissolution Act 1950 (Cth) was invalid. The Communist Party Case (1951) 83 CLR 1.

6. Krygger v. Williams, (1912) 15 CLR 366.

7. Kiorgaard v. Kiorgaard [1967] St.R.Qd.162.

8. Cf. Quick and Garren, Annotated Constitution of the Australian Constitution (1901). Sydney, 1901, p.951. It is also clear that there is no State religions of Australia and church and the State are separated. In a case in 1981 though the High Court took the view that the State aid to private religious schools (and in particular to the Catholic school system) provided through various items of Commonwealth State Grants legislation, was not in contrariety with Section 116; Attorney-General for Victoria; ex rel. Black v. The Commonwealth (1981) 55 ALJR 559.

unconstitutional. This throws the whole problem of determining which groups belong to such establishment or otherwise into the lap of local, State, Federal administration while granting or refusing to grant the financial privileges available.[9] In the D.O.G.s case the High Court held that the Commonwealth laws providing funds; in Territories directly and in States by Section 96 grants; for denominational schools were not "establishing any religion" within the meaning of Section 116 of the Federal Constitution.[10] Indeed due to these and other weaknesses of Section 116 a need is perceived for a Human Rights Bill ideally to be entrenched into the Federal Constitution.

B. Constitutional Guarantees of Freedom of Religion in South East Asia[11]

The aim of this section of the paper is to examine and contrast the Constitutional Guarantees of freedom as expounded in the Constitutions of Malaysia, Indonesia, Papua New Guinea and the Phillipines. Although these freedoms are supposedly guaranteed in these constitutions, it is doubtful whether freedom of religion exists in some of these countries.

---

9. ADB Report 1984, op.cit., p.53.

10. Op.cit., Black v. the Cth.

11. The views expressed in this section of the paper are the sole efforts of Mrs L.J. Mattingley.

MALAYSIA

Islam is the official religion of Malaysia, as opposed to Malaysia being an Islamic state.[12] The constitution expressly provides that other religions may be practiced in peace and harmony in any part of Malaysia.[13]

In recognition of the representation made by the rulers of the states, Article 3 Clause 2 was inserted to protect their position as the head of the Islamic religion in their respective states.[14] An assurance for the non-Muslim citizens was inserted in Article 3 Clause 3 to provide that their civil rights are not to be affected. Article 3 Clause 4 states that nothing in Article 3 derogates from any other provision of the constitution.

The basic freedoms of the constitution are found in Article 8, which provides that all persons are equal before the law and are entitled to the equal protection of the law,[15] except as expressly authorised by the constitution

---

12. Official Report of Legislative Council Debates, 1 May 1958, Columns 4631 and 4671-2.

13. Article 3 Clause 1 of the federal constitution of Malaysia proclaims that "Islam is the religion of the federation, but other religions may be practised in peace and harmony in any part of the federation."

14. Article 3 Clause 2, "In every state other than the states not having a Ruler the position of the ruler as the head of the Muslim religion in his state and the manner and to the extent acknowledged by the constitution of that state and subject to the constitution, all rights, privileges, prerogatives and powers enjoyed by him as head of that religion, are unaffected and unimpaired...".

15. Article 8 Clause 1.

discrimination against citizens on the ground of religion is prohibited.[16]

The Malaysian constitution generally seeks to prevent positive acts of discrimination by a governmental, or public body, as opposed to a private body. The forbidden governmental action may be either legislative or executive in nature. Furthermore, the constitution provides a number of exceptions to the general requirement of equality. For example, it is permissible for a law or practice to restrict office or employment connected with the affairs of any religion, or of an institution managed by a group professing any religion to persons professing that religion.[17] Discriminatory provisions in state constitutions which were in force immediately before the enactment of the federal constitution retain their validity.[18] Similarly, any new provision which corresponds to the ones which were previously in force will also be valid.

Article 11 of the Malaysian constitution provides that every person has the right to profess and practice his religion, subject to Article 11 Clause 4; which provides that a state law may control or restrict the propagation of any religious doctrine or belief among persons professing the Muslim religion.[19] No person may be compelled to pay any tax, the

---

16. Article 8 Clause 2.

17. Article 8 Clause 5(b).

18. Article 8(5)(e).

19. Enactments made under this Article are - Malacca Administration of Muslim Law Enactment 1959, Section 159(2).; Penang Administration of Muslim Law Enactment 1959, Section 157(2); Kedah Administration of Muslim Law

proceeds of which are specially allocated in whole or in part for the purposes of a religion other than his own.[20] Every religious group has the right to manage its own affairs, to establish and maintain institutions for religious or charitable purposes and to acquire and own property and hold and administer it in accordance with law.[21]

It is submitted that Article 11 is discriminatory in a number of respects. Firstly, the most obvious limitation relates to non-Muslims whose beliefs and religious practices include the propagation of their faith, for example Christianity. Secondly, religious freedom does not apply to Muslims since the state has power to deny them access to any other religious ideologies. With respect to enacted law, it is clear that it is not easy for a Muslim to abandon the practices of that faith. If a Muslim converts to another religion, he should be able to claim the religious freedom applicable to any other member of his new faith. On the other hand unfaithful acts while professing the Muslim religion will render him liable to criminal punishment.[22]

Article 12 provides in part that every religious group has the right to establish and maintain institutions for the education of children in its own religion, and there shall be

---

Enactment, 1962, Section 160(2); Kelantan Council of Religion and Malay Custom Enactment 1966, Section 68(2); Sabah Administration of Muslim Law Enactment 1977, Section 93A.

20. Article 11 Clause 2.

21. Article 11 Clause 4.

22. H.E. Groves, The Constitution of Malaysia, 1964, Malaysia Publications Ltd, Singapore, 1st edition, p.215.

no discrimination on the grounds only of religion in any law relating to such institutions or the administration of any such law; but it shall be lawful for the federation or a state to establish, maintain or assist in establishing an institution for the propagation of the Islamic religion.[23] This Article permits a government to appropriate such monies as it may deem necessary for the carrying into effect the instruction of the Islamic religion.[24]

It may be argued that Article 12 means that religious groups cannot establish schools except for the education of children in their own religion, but then it is difficult to comprehend why there cannot be discrimination in such institutions on the sole ground of religion. Article 12 Clause 3 provides that no person shall be required to participate in the worship of a religion other than his own and consequently he cannot be compelled to receive instruction in that faith. For the purposes of Clause 3 the religion of a person under the age of eighteen years shall be decided by his parents or guardians.[25]

Article 150 provides a power to act contrary to the provisions of the constitution. These powers are extensive

---

23. Article 12 Clause 2.

24. Article 11 Clause 2 provides that no person shall be compelled to pay any tax, the proceeds of which are specially allocated in whole or in part for the purposes of a religion other than his own". Therefore, any monies appropriated for this purpose must be collected from Muslims. It could be argued that this system of tax collecting and allocation of monies so obtained is open to abuse, especially in relation to monies collected from non-Muslims which may be put to use for Muslim purposes.

25. Article 12 Clause 4.

in scope except for certain restrictions.[26] Article 150 Clause 5 enables the Malaysian Parliament to make a law with respect to any matter notwithstanding anything contained in the constitution. This provision enables parliament to achieve directly under the pretext of emergency rule what it may not be able to do directly. This power is open to abuse by a government who wishes to discriminate against non-Muslims.

INDONESIA

On the other hand the Indonesian constitution of 1945 provides that the state shall be based upon belief in God the Almighty[27] and the state shall guarantee the freedom of every inhabitant to adhere to his own religion and make observance in accordance with such religion and belief.[28]

Approximately one hundred and twenty five of more than one hundred and thirty-five million Indonesians are officially listed as Muslims. In theory Indonesia is the worlds' largest Muslim society.[29] In reality approximately ten percent of statistical Muslims actually practice that faith.[30]

---

26. See Article 150 Clause 6A.

27. Chapter X Article 29(1).

28. Chapter X Article 29(2).

29. E. Utrecht "Army and Islamic Opposition in Indonesia (1979-80) 9-10 Journal of Contemporary Asia, p.175.

30. R.A.F. Paul Webb, Christians and Muslims in Indonesia; a Problem Solved? (1983) 12 Kabar Seberang 59. See generally R.A.F. Paul Webb, The Church in the Sandalwood Islands, 1960-1980. Occasional Paper No.4, James Cook University of North Queensland, p.1; R.A.F. Paul Webb, Indonesian

During the Japanese occupation of Indonesia the Japanese established an office for religious affairs. After the proclaimation of the Indonesian Republic "a ministry of religion" was created. This consisted of four sections - for Muslims, Protestants, Roman Catholics, and Hindu-Buddhists. It was established to basically support all sound, and proper religious movements, and to protect the same, as well as assuring freedom of religious belief and worship.

Since the foundation of the Republic, the Minister of Religious Affairs has been a Muslim politician. The Muslim population was annoyed by the appointment of a member of the military, namely General Alamsyah as Minister of Religious Affairs. It has been argued that it appears that the government was making concessions to former Sukarnists in order to enlist their support in the face of what is presented as a muslim problem.[31] Muslims feared that the government would recognise Kebatinan (Javanese mysticism) as an official religion, where as a true Muslim or Christian for that matter would regard "Kebatinan" as heresy.[32] On the other hand Indonesian Christians view the department as an outpost of militant Islam.[33]

Christians and their Political Parties. South East Asian Monograph Series, No.2, 1978, James Cook University of North Queensland, at p.1.

31. Professor Emeritus W.F. Wertheim, "Muslims in Indonesia: Majority with Minority Mentality." Occasional Paper No.8, James Cook University of North Queensland at p.14.

32. E. Utrecht, op.cit., p.183.

33. Op.cit., p.183.

In 1978, the Minister of Religious Affairs Dr General Alamsyah introduced two ordinances, namely the first and second decisions, both of which discriminate against non-Muslim religions. The first decision stated that no church or religious building may be erected where there were complaints from local residents. In 1981 a Chinese area of Jakarta sought permission for the erection of a small buddhist temple; this permission was refused because two or three Muslims objected.[34] The second decision concerned proselytizing. A person may not in law give a bible to a neighbour because that would be considered to be proselytizing, but on the other hand to give a Koran to a neighbour is not proselytizing.

Further inroads into the freedom of religion will be made when the law on social organizations[35] is passed in mid-1986. This Act will require all organizations affiliated with any of the state recognized religions to subscribe to the offical state formula, Panca Sila,[36] as the sole basis of their existence.[37] A social organization may not engage

---

34. R.A.F. Paul Webb, op.cit., at p.62; In Irian Jaya, where there never were Muslims and where the population was Christian or animist in nearly every village there stands a mosque.

35. For a detailed discussion of the effect of this Act, together with an interpretation of the draft legislation see Peter Burns; The Decline of Freedom of Religion in Indonesia. Centre for Southeast Asian Studies, Occasional paper No.21, James Cook University of North Queensland, Townsville.

36. These are the five 'pillars' of the Indonesian state; belief in one God, nationalism, humanitarism, democracy and social justice.

37. See Section 2(1) of the Act.

in political activities[38] and the government is able to exercise supervision over the social organizations.[39] If the Act is not challenged on constitutional grounds, there is a real possibility that the constitutional guarantee of freedom of religion will be a thing of the past.

PAPUA NEW GUINEA

The constitution of Papua New Guinea provides that every person has the right to freedom of conscience, thought and religion[40] and the practice of his religion subject to a number of exceptions. For example, no person can be compelled to receive religious instruction, but a child may receive the same with the consent of his parents,[41] and no person is entitled to intervene unsolicited into the affairs of a person of a different belief,[42] and no person may be compelled to take an oath which is contrary to his own religion.[43] It is interesting to note[44] the purpose for which this section was drafted. It allows those persons who are Christians or who belong to any other religion links with

---

38. See Section 12 of the Act.

39. Section 14(1).

40. See Section 45.

41. See Section 45(2).

42. See Section 45(3).

43. See Section 45(4).

44. A reference in Section 45 to religion includes a reference to the traditional religious beliefs and customs of the peoples of Papua New Guinea - Section 45(5).

their traditional practices and beliefs. This explains the emphasis on the exercise of rights to propagate religious views only to the extent that they do not interfere with the freedom of others.[45]

THE PHILLIPINES

The constitution of the Phillipines expresses the right to the free exercise of religion in broader terms than any of the preceeding constitutions. Section 8 of Article 4 of the Bill of Rights states that:

> "No law shall be made respecting an establishment of religion or prohibiting the free exercise thereof. The free exercise and enjoyment of religious profession and worship without discrimination or preference, shall forever be allowed. No religious test shall be required for the exercise of civil or political rights."

This section prohibits a law respecting the establishment of religion. This has been interpreted to mean that no religious sect shall be favoured by the state or given an advantage by law over other sects.[46] A state cannot openly or secretly participate in the affairs of any religious organization or group and vice versa.[47] This section also prohibits the state employing its facilities or funds in a way that gives any church greater strength than it would have had, by relying on its members alone.

---

45. J. Goldring, The Constitution of Papua New Guinea, 1978, The Law Book Co. Ltd, 1st edition, Sydney.

46. Emerson v. Board of Education (1947) 330 U.S.1.

The second prohibition contained in Section 8 relates to laws prohibiting the free exercise of religion. Its effect is to protect the freedom of belief, ritual, education and proselytizing. Essentially religious belief is protected by prohibiting the government from requiring an individual to hold a particular kind of religious belief or punish him because he belongs to a minority religion. Religious ritual is protected by prohibiting the government from singling out religious ritual for prohibiting ritual. Religious education is protected by preventing the state from insisting that all children be given a secular public education. Religious proselytizing is protected by setting out such limits as are allowed with other kinds of speech.

The Phillipines' society is predominantly Christian, although a Muslim population does exist. The Islam professed is far from being orthodox and is Islam in name and form, more than it is in substance.[48] On the 4th day of February, 1977 President Marcos brought into being a presidential decree No.1083 which was a new "Code of Muslim Personal Laws of the Phillipines". The code is arranged in five books totalling one hundred and ninety Articles covering the following areas, persons and family relations, succession, settlement of disputes and the giving of legal opinions, penal provisions and transaction provisions: it took effect from the date of its promulgation and it represents a

---

47. Albington Township (Pa) v. Schempp (1963) 83 Sup.Ct.1560.

48. Melvin Mednick "Sultans and Mayors" in Gowing and McAmis (eds), The Muslim Filipinos, Manila, 1974, Solidaridad Publishing House, pp.225-9 at p.226.

definitive statement of the law applicable to the Muslims of the Phillipines.[49]

It should be noted that this new law is not a codification of existing principles, but is something completely new. It appears that the law has been largely extracted from the Shafi'i law relating to marriage, divorce, maintenance and succession. Because of the nature of the Muslim in the Phillipines, it is an introduction of "Islamic" legal principles rather than a codification of existing law.[50]

The religious freedom expounded in the constitution of the Phillipines[51] is expressed in wider terms than that which is promulgated in the Malaysian and Indonesian constitutions. This may be attributable to the difference in cultures. In Malaysia for example the Islamic religion itself poses a type of barrier between Muslims and the other religions, since it forbids marriage between Muslim women and non-Muslim men.

On the other hand the freedom of religion expressed in the constitution of Papua New Guinea has some features which are analogous to that of the Malaysian constitution. It also permits the native population to enjoy a religion of their own choosing as well as continuing to practice their tribal beliefs.

<u>49.</u> M.B. Hooker, Islamic Law in South East Asia, Oxford University Press, 1984, Singapore, 1st edition at p.231.

<u>50.</u> M.B. Hooker, op.cit., at p.232.

<u>51.</u> Regulating the only Asian country which is predominantly Christian.

It should come as no surprise to learn that Malaysia, Indonesia, and Papua New Guinea have not ratified the International Convention on Civil and Political Rights.[52] The Phillipines has ratified the ICCPR as well as the optional protocol to the ICCPR.[53] It should be noted that it is highly probable that the Phillipines will obtain a new constitution in the foreseeable future as a result of Mrs Aquino coming to power.

C. International Convention on Civil and Political Rights[54]

Australia ratified the ICCPR of 1976 in 1980 with certain reservations. Article 18 of the Covenant spells out the right of freedom of religion and the right to practise it. It reads as follows:

"1. Everyone shall have the right to freedom of thought, conscience and religon. This right shall include freedom to have or to adopt a religion or belief of his choice, and freedom, either individually or in community with others and in public or private, to manifest his religion or belief in worship, observance, practice and teaching.

2. No one shall be subject to coercion which would impair his freedom to have or to adopt a religion or belief of his choice.

---

52. Hereinafter referred to as the ICCPR.

53. T.B. Millar, Current International Treaties, Croom and Helm, Sydney, 1st edition, 1984, pp.546-548.

54. Hereinafter referred to as ICCPR.

3. Freedom to manifest one's religion or beliefs may be subject only to such limitations as are prescribed by law and are necessary to protect public safety, order, health, or morals or the fundamental rights and freedoms of others.

4. The States Parties to the present Covenant undertake to have respect for the liberty of parents and, when applicable, legal guardians to ensure the religious and moral education of their children in conformity with their own convictions."

Consequently the Human Rights Commission Act 1981 (Cth) was enacted by the Fraser government. This Act annexed the ICCPR and established the Commission in December 1981. By annexing the ICCPR the Commission is given the power to investigate complaints of a breach of human rights contained in the ICCPR. Religious freedom is now justiciable in a tribunal with some powers.

ICCPR in Other Countries

We are nearly in the next century and need to change our attitudes to accommodate this change. Whereas Britain has some form of Bill of Rights (as Britain is subject to the European Convention on Human Rights) and the rights are enforceable in a court of law namely the European Court, Australia does not have any that emanates from a treaty obligation and which can be enforced in any court of law. Whereas in the United States, the Bill of Rights and particularly the right to due process[55] has enabled the Supreme Court of the United States to extend the major guarantees of the Bill of Rights to cover State legislation by expounding the implicit requirements of liberty and due process. Australia has no equivalent of the 'due process' clause. The concept of due process in its substantive form has also been applied to strengthen the important rights enshrined in the Fifth Amendment.[56] It shouldf Britain being

sed to the European Convention and a European Court on Human Rights, a Bill of Rights Bill was introduced by Lord Wade in the House of Lords which required similar legislation to be construed subject to the European Convention on Human Rights. Lord Scarman introduced a Bill to bring the European rights into the English Court of Municipal Law. While such developments are taking place in Britain and while similar civil liberties were protected through a Human Rights Bill in Canada (another Commonwealth country) more than a decade ago the Liberal attitudes to civil liberties and the Bill of Rights puts Australia more than a decade back in history. The Indian Constitution protects human rights describing them as "fundamental rights". They are enforceable and entrenched in the constitution (though eclipsed by the declaration of emergency) and not to be removed from the constitution even

---

55. The stipulation of the Fourteenth Amendment to the United States Constitution that no State shall deprive any person of life, liberty or property without due process of law.

56. T.R.S. Allan, "Legislative Supremacy and the Rule of Law, Democracy and Constitutionalism" 1985 Cambridge Law Journal, p.111.

by a constitutional amendment. In this regard the Indian judicial approach is similar to the United States'. The two greatest democracies in the world, whether in terms of population or in terms of area, are providing sufficient argument and example for the States with written constitutions as opposed to countries like South Africa; where either there are no written guarantees of any sort or human rights are put in jeopardy by successive regimes.

Optional Protocol to the ICCPR

Australia has been consistently hesitant in acceding to the Optional Protocol to the ICCPR. Even Senator Gareth Evans believes that adoption of the Protocol involves the State Party recognising the competence of the Human Rights Committee to receive and consider communications from individuals subject to its jurisdiction who claim to be victims of a violation by that State Party of any of the rights set forth in the Covenant. He believed, and shared this view at that time with the Minister for Foreign Affairs Mr Bill Hayden that adoption of the Optional Protocol would enhance Australia's reputation relating to international human rights by demonstrating a readiness to submit our human rights performance to further international scrutiny.[57] Australia has not acceded to the Optional Protocol of the Covenant. It leads to the conclusion that the anticipated enhancement of Australia's international human rights reputation has not been accomplished. Taking the argument a

---

57. G. Evans, 1984, Australian Foreign Affairs Record, 324.

step further _a fortiori_ Australia's reluctance to sign and accede to the Protocol lowers Austalia's international human rights reputation.

The second issue relates to a companion proposal to the Optional Protocol concerning the making by Australia of a declaration under Article 41 of the ICCPR. Under this Article a State Party to the ICCPR may declare that it recognises the competence of the Human Rights committee to receive and consider communications to the effect that a State Party claims that another State Party is not fulfilling its obligations under the Covenant. Communications under Article 41 may be received and considered only if submitted by a State Party which has made a declaration recognising in regard to itself the competence of the Human Rights Committee. He mentions that only fourteen of the seventy-five States parties to the ICCPR have made the declaration under Article 14 as compared with the twenty-nine that have ratified the Optional Protocol. Australia is amongst those who have not ratified the Protocol but has made the declaration. We share Mr Evan's views that by making a declaration under Article 41 Australia would be making a public commitment concerning the ICCPR and its willingness to allow our human rights records to be scrutinised by other countries. This would merely give formal legal expression to what is already this government's position in relation to the ICCPR.[58]

---

58. G. Evans, ibid, at p.328.

D. Human Rights Commission

The establishment of a Human Rights Commission (HRC) was a major development for the protection of rights and freedoms. However the Human Rights Commission Act 1981 provides in Section 36 that it automatically ceases five years after its date of commencement. The Human Rights Commission also has functions under the Racial Discrimination Act 1975 and the Sex Discrimination Act 1984. These functions include educational and promotional activities, reporting on legislation or practices that may be inconsistent with human rights, and attempting to settle complaints through conciliation.[59] The Human Rights Commission has jurisdiction to examine existing Commonwealth, ACT or External Territory laws and it must forward a report to the Minister. Such a report is to be made public by being laid before each House of Parliament within 15 sitting days of receipt thereof. In four years the Human Rights Commission has produced nearly a dozen reports.[60] Although under the unamended Human Rights Commission Act the action on

---

59. A Bill of Rights for Australia? Exposure Report by the Senate Standing Committee on Constitutional and Legal Affairs, AGPS Canberra 1985, p.19.

60. It also produces a Newsletter, Occasional Papers, Discussion Papers and other teaching material. In a historic report for example the Human Rights commission opined that decision such as those of deportation must conform with human rights. The Commission followed Bhajan Singh's case [1975] 3 W.L.R. 225 (at p.231 per Denning M.R.) where it was held that, though the European Convention for the Protection of Human Rights and Fundamental Freedoms is not brought into observance by subjecting it to an Act of Parliament; the European Convention 'can and should' be taken into account by the Court. The Commission said, the "Australian case law, in its current state of development, has failed to assimilate human rights law to any significant extent." Human Rights Commission Report No:3 at p.8.

a complaint does not go beyond a report to the Minister. Under the other two Acts it is impossible for an individual discriminated against in ways made unlawful by the Acts, ultimately to obtain court orders. When conducting inquiries the Human Rights Commission has power under each of the three Acts to compel persons to participate in the procedure. The Human Rights Commission protects the freedom of religion through, inter alia, Article 18 of ICCPR relating to right to freedom of thought, conscience and religion. The Canadian Charter of Rights and Freedom compared with the Australian Human Rights Commission Act "guarantees the rights and freedoms only to such reasonable limits prescribed by law as can be demonstrably justified in a free democratic society."[61] The ICCPR approaches the question of qualifications to the rights by a general provision in Article 4 "in time of public emergency which threatens the life of the nation." It also attaches specific derogation provisions on an article-by-article basis to most of the rights and freedoms which are set out in the Covenant.

The Racial Discrimination Act 1975 is founded on the International Convention on the Elimination of All Forms of Racial Discrimination. This Convention does not cover religious discrimination. However, Article 20 of the ICCPR and Principle 10 of the Declaration of the Rights of the Child both cover religious hatred together with racial hatred as different facets of a single phenomenon. Article 20 is particularly explicit in providing that 'any advocacy of

---

61. Section 1 of the Canadian Charter of Rights and Freedoms.

national, racial or religious hatred that constitutes incitement to discrimination, hostility or violence shall be prohibited by law'. If the Racial Discrimination Act were to be amended to cover discrimination on the grounds of religion, such an amendment should clearly apply to the Act as a whole and not simply to the provisions concerning hatred and incitement.

It was suggested by the Human Rights Commission that the statements inciting religious hatred and defamation of religious groups should be unlawful but it considered that the Racial Discrimination Act is not an appropriate place for such a provision. The Commission noted that Australia fully supported the adoption of the Declaration on the Elimination of All Forms of Intolerance and of Discrimination based on Religious Belief and considers that further action on this issue should be based on that Declaration. It argued that the failure to cover discrimination association with religion results in some highly undesirable inequities. If Jews are to be considered as an ethnic group (as they are regarded in New Zealand) then Jews but not Muslims would be protected. If, on the other hand, being Jewish is regarded as a religious rather than an ethnic affiliation then anti-semitism is excluded from the scope of the legislation. Section 116 of the Australian Constitution prevents the Federal Government from establishing a religion but does not appear to preclude legislation outlawing religious discrimination.[62] It is further argued that if religious

62. Cf. Jehovah's Witnesses Case, op.cit. In this the High Court _inter alia_ held that the non-cooperation of a

discrimination is not to be included within the framework of the Racial Discrimination Act, one possible alternative would be to include a very broad definition of freedom of religion in the proposed Bill of Rights.

> "This solution, however would leave unresolved the problem of incitement to religious hatred. At present religious hatred is an issue for Jews and, to a lesser extent, Muslims. Almost half of the most serious complaints of group defamation received by the Commission relates to rabid anti-semitic propaganda. If racial defamation alone were to be covered by the amended legislation then there is a strong probability that those persons who deliberately inflame inter-community tensions in Australia would shift the focus of their attack to the religious affiliations of Asians, Jews and other minorities. British experience has shown that this is not a merely hypothetical prospect. The racist journals which once attacked Indians and Brownskins now use Hindu as an extreme term of abuse."[63]

E. Executive Power and Religion

It was recommended by the Senate Standing committee on Constitutional Affairs in its Exposure Report that the inherent executive capacity to act should be subject to a

---

particular group wth the Commonwealth's defence effort as excluding that group from the immunity provided by Section 116 of the Federal Constitution.

63. Human Rights Report No:7 (1984) A.G.P.S., pp.17-18.

Bill of Rights.[64] Such inherent executive capacity does not have any legislative backing. It does not have the power to issue orders backed by enforceable sanctions, nor the power to override common law or statutory rights.[65] However there are examples where it can legitimately interfere with fundamental rights and freedoms.[66] Although the Crown prerogative to conscript may well no longer exist,[67] wartime legislation without any constitutional guarantee will not save any conscientious objector from service on the basis of his religion. Australia needs a human rights bill because the Royal Prerogatives are very wide in Australia. Barton v. The Commonwealth[68] departed from De Keyser's case[69] thereby giving preference to Royal Prerogative over statute. It could be argued that the 'monarch', with the help of Barton, can contravene any Bill of Rights. In this respect John Goldring's[70] conclusion on the Royal Prerogative may be stated as follows:

> "The legislation on human rights which the present Commonwealth government proposed may be a step in

---

64. Op.cit., at p.59.

65. Op.cit., p.58. Cf. A rival view is expressed in J. Golding "The Impact of Statute on the Royal Prerogative" (1974) Australian Law Journal, p.434.

66. Church of Scientology v. Woodward (1982) 43 ALR 587.

67. Marks v. Commonwealth (1964) 111 CLR 549. Cf. Op.cit., Krygger v. Williams.

68. (1974) 48 ALJR 161.

69. (1920) AC 508.

70. Op.cit., at p.442.

> this direction, but given the indications contained in Barton's case that any statute which is alleged to limit the prerogative will be construed strictly by the Courts, the possibility remains that the legislation may be held by the courts not to disclose specifically and unambiguously an intention to curtail or displace areas of the prerogative to the extent contemplated, according to the broad aims of the draftsmen of the legislation."

These words of caution still hold some validity and should be taken into account when laying down the final model of the Bill of Rights.[71]

F. <u>Religion and the Defence of Realm</u>

The general argument that fair laws be written, published and be predictable apply equally to human rights. They need to be spelt out in a Federal State with a written constitution more than in a unitary form of government for they provide unity, uniformity and harmony amongst the people of the states joining as a federation. The absence of such rights is felt more in emergent situations when for example the internment of 'enemy aliens' takes place. Australia, like Canada, being a country of migrants, needs to have an open ended declared policy on internees who should be subject to international scrutiny. A Lebanese Muslim migrating to Australia, for example, does not know what rights he may have

---

<u>71.</u> With the utmost respect to the Crown the moral is that we need to put this 'royal genie' back in the bottle; but the question is how?

if he is interned in case Libya (without in any way supporting her actions) declares war against Australia or vice versa. Take the example of a second generation Indonesian Muslim settled in Australia who may be interned if Indonesia was to declare war against Australia. The precendents of the Second World War; when Italians, Germans and other enemy aliens were interned in Australia; should not be used as an argument to treat all migrants as fifth columnists.[72]

Muslims have always enjoyed a special place in Australia. Due to the Afghan pioneers the second religious group to enjoy their places of worship were Muslims. Up to recent times Muslims whichever country they came from enjoyed special treatment. The Turks for example were never interned during the First World War and no reprisal was reported against them in the recent past or during the pre-Federation period. Such a record may be attributable to the attitude and religious beliefs of Muslims in Australia. Due to events and happenings in certain Muslim countries, there were certain repercussions in the U.S. Although it is true to say that Australia has not always followed the American example in how to treat their Muslim counterparts, these attitudes are determined by diplomatic and economic rather than legal considerations. In the light of historical events and judici al norms the question of the defence power of the Federation requires further elaboration. Although the High Court has

---

72. Under Regulation 20 of National Security (Aliens Control) Regulations of 1939 (No.88) legislated under National Security Act 1939-1943 which, along with the regulations, was repealed on 31 December 1946.

rejected the view that the exclusive power of defence vests in the federal government, there are some aspects specifically exclusive, that is, raising of armed forces (Section 114), control of armed forces and defence departments (Section 69 and Section 52(ii)) and the prerogative of declaring war and peace (inter alia, Section 68 and 70).[73] However a question whether the High Court will accept the maxim salus populi supreme lex cannot be answered. The defence power changes during peace or ostensible peace time, intermediate period (i.e. prior to war or during period of considerable international tension) and war time. It is an undeniable fact that the Commonwealth has been able to exercise a great degree of legal control in war time under the defence power and that the cases in which it has been denied have been few in number and relatively unimportant in context.[74] "Secondary aspects" of the defence power provide unfettered powers to the Federation. The defence of a country is particularly the concern of the Executive and in war the exigencies are many, varied and so urgent, that width and generality are a characteristic of the powers which it must exercise.[75] The defence power even in peace time authorises any legislation which is reasonably

---

73. Carter v. Egg & Egg Pulp Marketing Board (1942) 66 CLR 557.

74. For further discussion on the subject see Sugarman, B. & Dignam, W.J. "The Defence Power and Total War", (1943) 17 Australian Law Journal 207 and Sawyer, G. "The Defence Power of the Commonwealth in Time of War", (1946) 20 Australian Law Journal 295. Cf. Gordon Borrie, "Court Martial, Civilians, and Civil Liberties", (1969) 32 Modern Law Review, pp.35-52.

75. per Dixon J., Wishart v. Fraser (1941) 64 CLR 470.

necessary to prepare for war, including legislation which would be authorised by an expansion of the power in view of the increasing probability of imminent war.[76] As a consequence of thes views of the superior judiciary it is imperative that specific statutory guarantees be made available to the migrants generally and specifically non-Christian religions against any war time reprisals under legislation like National Security Act or Defence Preparation Act. It is imperative because common law in Australia is not regarded as secular and Christian religion is regarded as part of common law.[77]

G. The Bill of Rights Bill, 1985[78]

It is desirable that a Bill of Rights should be a higher law in terms of which the validity of other laws would have to be judged.[79] The rights and freedoms stated in the BORB are those rights and freedoms internationally recognized as the minimum standards to which government should conform in dealing with individuals within their jurisdictions.[80] It is noteworthy that the BORB contains no guarantees of freedom

---

76. Communist Party Case, ibid, per Williams J.

77. Cowan v. Milbourn [1867] L.R. 2 Ex.234 per Kelly C.B. It may be noted, however, that the word 'religion' has been defined by the High Court in very wide sense and may include all non-Christian faiths. Church of New Faith v. Commissioner of Payroll Tax (Vic.) 83 ATC 4652

78. Hereinafter referred to as the BORB.

79. G. Palmer, A Bill of Rights for Australia. Social Alternatives, Vol.5, No.1, November 1985 at p.6.

80. Second Reading Speech in the Senate, by Senator the Hon. John Button, Minister representing the Attorney-General, in the Senate, on the Australian Bill of Rights Bill, 1985.

of information, and there is no reference to a minimum level of health and social services. There is however a right to vote,[81] a right to life,[82] liberty and security.[83] A host of legal rights ensure due procedures of the law[84] as well as forbidding the application of retrospective legislation.[85] The fundamental freedoms of conscience[86] and religion[87] peaceful assembly[88] and association[89] are listed.

Given the modern mobility of labour, certain mobility rights are set down to enable every Australian to move freely from one state or territory to another.[90] An important qualification to the BORB is what is known as a 'notwithstanding clause", which essentially means that the Commonwealth Government can derogate from the BORB providing it expressly states this in the relevant Act.[91]

---

81. Article 6(b).

82. Article 18.

83. Article 19.

84. Articles 20-32.

85. Article 28.

86. Article 8.

87. Article 9.

88. Article 10.

89. Article 11.

90. Article 15(1).

91. Section 12. On the other hand in the Canadian Charter of Rights and Freedoms this course of action is available to the federal and provincial legislature notwithstanding the fact that such provisions are valid only for five years. To extend their duration it is necessary to review and repeat the express declaration. Dr H.C.J. Phillips, Social Sciences Forum, (1983) Vol.9 No.2, December, p.1 at p.2.)

The provisions of the ICCPR are not enforceable in Australia despite the fact that Australia has ratified it. To be made enforceable it must form part of our domestic law.[92] The optional protocol which allows individuals to make complaints under the covenant has not been signed by Australia. The covenant itself specifically commits Australia to adopting legislative measures to give effect to the rights it contains.[93] Senator Gareth Evans has stated that the covenant has been adopted by a large number of countries. For example, the United Kingdom has signed and ratified the covenant, in spite of also being one of the first signatories to the European convention which essentially covers the same ground as the ICCPR. He further stated that New Zealand has ratified the covenant and is in fact moving to a statutory Bill of rights.[94] Canada has ratified the covenant[95] and now has a constitutional charter of rights.[96] The commonwealth government also intends to pass a Bill which will have the effect of reforming and improving the Human Rights Commission, which if passed will be renamed and reconstituted as the Human Rights and Equal Opportunities Commission. A majority of the states have legislated in the areas of equal opportunities, sex discrimination, and race relations. The commonwealth

---

92. Hence the need to introduce and pass the BORB.

93. See Article 2(2) of the ICCPR.

94. G. Palmer, op.cit., at p.6.

95. Dr H.C.J. Phillips, op.cit.

96. Senator Gareth Evans, Senate - Questions without notice, 13 February, 1986, p.2621.

government hopes to sign agreements with the Northern Territory and Queensland after these jurisdictions have passed legislation governing human rights and equal opportunities. Existing state cooperative arrangements will continue under the new commission.[97]

H. Conclusion

Whereas it may appear that the present Labor government is proposing more vigorous Human Rights legislation than former governments. It viewed in a historical perspective, it can be demonstrated that this is an inaccurate assessment. It is instructive to compare the Human Rights Bill 1973 (the then Senator Lionel Murphy's proposal) with the Human Rights and Equal Opportunity Commission Bill 1984 (Senator Gareth Evan's proposal). Both of these Bills are the products of one-time Labor Attorneys-General. The Bill of Rights Bill 1985 at least on the question of religious freedom is substantially similar to the 1984 Bill. The comparison is instructive because at least two differences are evident. Firstly the provisions of the 1973 Bill provided for judicial review and enforcement, while the 1984 Bill provided for only executive review and enforcement. Secondly the approach of the 1973 Bill was to define protected rights and freedoms, as opposed to the 1984 Bill which merely continued the current role of the Human Rights Commission under a broadened title of ensuring that the United Nations Covenants are respected at the Commonwealth level.

---

97. Second Reading Speech, op.cit., at p.4.

It is submitted that due to these differences the former Bill reflected a more vigorous attitude, by it people were to be permitted to see what rights and freedoms they had and could then themselves enforce them. The 1984 Bill did not contain either of these factors, but instead appears to do more for the individual than tell them that somewhere, there is a Commission that is protecting them, but that they cannot protect themselves. Consequently the people have no designated role in the area of human rights. It has been noted that human rights are being embroiled in politics. Given the differences indicated above it is hoped that the intention of the present Labor government to pass fresh human rights legislation, even though it may be mitigated, is not itself a mere political gesture, but rather a positively humane expression of rights.

General Conclusions

It may be reiterated that the most desirable means to achieve the human rights goal is to entrench them in the Federal Constitution.[98]

---

98. This view is the view of Mr P. Buttar only.